By His Touch

A True to Life Personal Account of Miraculous Healing and Renewed Faith

Rolando Y. Dy Buco

Hyena Press
Los Altos, CA
www.HyenaPress.com

This book is published by Hyena Press.
2310 Homestead Rd, C1 #125
Los Altos, CA
www.HyenaPress.com

Printed and bound in the United States of America.

First Paperback Edition

ISBN 978-0-9842239-2-3

Book Design: Thomas White
Editing: George Joseph

ATTENTION CHURCHES, ORGANIZATIONS
—DISCOUNT ON BULK PURCHASES AVAILABLE.

For information, please contact the publisher:
www.HyenaPress.com,
info@hyenapress.com, (408) 329-4597

For my loving wife, *Mariquit*,
who shared with me the vision of Perfect Love
that we have experienced in an imperfect world.

Map of the Philippines

Basco
Batan Islands

Babuyan Islands

Claveria
Aparri
Laoag
Tuao · Tuguegarao
Vigan
Ilagan
· Bontoc
Planan
San Fernando
Cabarroguis
Bolinao
Baguio   Casiguran
Dagupan
Lingayen
San Jose   Baler
Luzon   Tarlac
Iba   Cabanatuan

Polillo Islands
Polillo
Manila

Daet
Catanduanes Islands
Plaridel   Sipocot
Boac   Pili   Virac
Mamburao   Calapan   Legaspi
San Pascual   Sorsogon
Bongabong   Matnog
Mindoro
Romblon   Catarman   Samar
Busuanga Island   Calbayog
San Jose   Catbalogan
Calamian Group   Kalibo   Borongan
Roxas   Danao
Culasi   Panay   Tacloban
Cadiz   Ormoc
San Jose   Iloilo   Visayan Islands   Leyte
Toledo   Danao
Dumaran   La Carlota   Cebu   Maasin
Cebu   Antao
Palawan   Bohol   Pilar
Puerto Princesa   Negros   Bais   Tagbilaran   Cortes
Dumaguete   Siquijor   Mambajao
Dapitan   Butuan
Gingoog   Prosperidad
Ozamis   Iligan   Bislig
Pagadian   Mindanao
Tagum
Olutanga   Davao   Mati
Zamboanga   Maganoy   Digos   Governor Generoso
Isulan   Koronadal
General Santos
Jolo   Jose Abad Santos
Jolo Island
Tawitawi Island
Balimbing

Philippines

Kalibo
Roxas
Culasi   Panay   Vis
San Jose   Iloilo   Ca
La Carlota   Tol

Contents

PREFACE

Why are we here? What is the purpose of life?
Where should one go to look for the answers to these fundamental questions about life?

I am your ordinary person. I am not so differently built than the guy standing beside me in a street corner while waiting for the green light to turn red.

We both express cool indifference to what's happening around us as we hurriedly step on the familiar stripes painted white across the road. But surely, our individual answers to the same old questions about life may contain disparate wisdoms that could make us distinctly different from each other.

At life's end no one will ask me how many college degrees I have, how many condominium units I own, or how many expensive cars are parked in my garage. Men are doomed to run after values that eventually become zero in the end.

Now, I know better. I am here with the mandate **to learn** as much as I could about life. My second mandate is not to wander away from my life's purpose **to love** without limit.

How do I know this? Depths of experience lead me to answers.

Only *By His Touch* were my eyes opened to the intrinsic value of my own life spent on earth, enriched by God's nurturing love and shared with beings built exactly like me.

The next guy standing beside me in a street corner while waiting for the green light to turn red may have his own story to tell.

Here is mine.

"Love cannot save life from death, but it can fulfill life's purpose."
-Arnold Toynbee

INTRODUCTION

Do you believe in miracles?
What would it take for you to believe in one?

Life is a jigsaw puzzle. We spend time putting it together, hoping to create a complete picture out of all the scattered pieces. Sometimes it seems as if a piece is missing as you are left frustrated and confused. You almost reach the point of surrender and hunt for renewed challenge elsewhere. But the urge to do more is hard to resist.

Surely we have been pursuing the wrong pieces to the puzzle as our desire to re-create haunts us. At some point, all the pieces suddenly fit into place; just as quickly, however, your level of elation for having accomplished something fizzles out, not unlike a momentary flash of cordite that illuminates the night sky.

Is this all there is to it?

I was ushered into questions about my own existence as I approached the peak of my career curve. The trappings of success and my intense focus on material pursuits did not erase the deep loneliness I felt upon looking closely at myself and evaluating my identity.

Who am I? Where am I going? Am I truly destined to go anywhere else?

It wasn't long before I came to realize that my doubts were anchored in my own hidden deep-seated fears. I feared about the unknown so much that I got so terrified about dying. I was afraid of facing my insignificance and sense of insecurity. I was frightened to confront the failure to resolve the issues I have tried my best to square away for a long time. I harbored a restless soul in search of my Sabbath.

Then one November, in the year 1991, *it* happened.

My daughter, Shasha, was only 15 years old at the time. She had been suffering from severe headaches for a while. Soon, she started experiencing extreme heaviness in her head.

What could this be?

Imagine your beloved child complaining of such symptoms in a region as critical to life as the brain. A parent's initial reactions would be much concern mixed with fear and terror. This was our baby who was suffering, but my wife and I could do little to ease her pain. The helplessness was crippling.

November 8, 1991, was the day when our lives began to change forever.

This was the day when Shasha was diagnosed with Communicating Hydrocephalus. It is a condition where the brain's cerebrospinal fluid gets trapped in the skull, unable to drain away through the body's natural channels in place.

Our daughter's brain was being compressed by its own life-supporting fluids.

Not only did this explain my daughter's headaches and feelings of heaviness, but this condition also brought to light some of our worst fears. Communicating Hydrocephalus causes more than just discomfort. It is a condition that can also lead to impaired brain functions and development, convulsions, and even mental retardation.

The horror-filled week that started on November 8, 1991, was the most difficult week we went through as a family. Further, as it turned out, it was also our most joyous and blessed week—one that we will never ever forget.

I was not a soundly religious person up to that point in time. My expression of faith was based more on obligation and convention, not one rooted in true belief. It was in this state of faith (or lack of it) that I found myself reacting to the facts of life with deep-seated fears

Unexpectedly, during the days immediately following her diagnosis, my daughter began having powerful spiritual experiences. She started to enter trance states where she would claim to be in direct communication with what can best be described as divine sources.

Then, a miracle happened. Within the week, while receiving a series of these profoundly transforming spiritual messages, Shasha was healed. Consequently, my perspective on life and faith was permanently altered, my moral compass re-directed, and I too began to be healed.

By His Touch we are made whole.

God is inscrutable and ineffable. We are blessed to know about Him from His own revelations through symbols familiar to man. He is revealed as the fire of the burning bush. Or as the blinding presence of light in the Scriptures. Or as the healing force.

It was His visage as fire that ignited the restlessness of my inner life and gave me focus. He granted me light to direct me to where to lay down my burdens, heal my hurts, expose my grief and affirm my brokenness. My family and I experienced God's presence as the Divine Healer of our physical and spiritual infirmities in perfect time. That made us feel enfolded in a celestial embrace, forgiven and sufficiently fuelled for the long journey ahead.

I personally went through a cleansing miracle that transformed my doubts into a spiritual fruit I aim to share with you. I am not a duly ordained fire-breathing evangelist of our time. But, the dynamism of that healing process continues to breathe life and throb with ardor inside my soul. This true story keeps energizing thousands, and provides the spark needed for their incipient spiritual maturity to advance.

Every time something like this takes place, a *miracle* happens. Then, we find healing and we doubt no more.

"Then Jesus told him, 'Because you have seen me, you have believed; blessed are those who have not seen and yet have believed'."

–John 20:29

Within this book are my personal accounts, reflections, and inspired writings concerning my family's and my transformative journey to wholeness.

The book is divided into three main parts. **Part I** consists of several separate documents written on different dates. Each document recalls the many different events surrounding Shasha's miraculous healing. The chapter entitled *The First Document* was written on November 16, 1991 and chronicles the days leading up to this extraordinary event. The second chapter, *The Days After*, is a set of personal accounts written on the days following immediately afterwards. The third chapter, *Blessed Returns*, is a personal reflection written years later, on May 23, 2004.

My original purpose of writing down what happened was purely personal in nature. I wanted to keep my recollection fresh about what took place. The event was a life-changing phenomenon for my family and me. It came easy for me to write things down as I felt the force of inspiration too over-powering to ignore. There were times when I was having goose bumps while writing down the account at night while sometimes I was left alone in the house.

The second part of the book, **Part II**, contains my personal reflections 18 years after the wondrous occurrences of 1991. It is here where I reflect upon the trials and tribulations of my life, the birth of my renewed faith, my appreciation for the grace of God, and my renewed relationship with the Holy Spirit.

Part III consists of personal reflections and original poetry duly inspired by my life experiences.

I was moved by the Holy Spirit to place my personal writings into a book. I have set no self-serving goals or aspirations for this undertaking. It will never be my intention to make money or attempt to transform other people regarding their religious leanings or affiliation through this book. I was simply moved by the Spirit – *inspired* – to place my writings in a format that could be easily shared.

However, many readers of my story in its original manuscript form, given away free inside and outside of the Philippines during the past 20 years or so, have expressed their inner resurgence of their faith in God. This is true even today.

So now, my hope for you is spiritual transformation and the renewal of spiritual outlook, if you are in need of it. This was exactly what the experience did to me.

I wish for you to find inspiration from this book and pray that you become more joyful about re-discovering the reality of God. I, together with my family, remain a living witness to, and participant in, this wonderful experience of perfect love.

"He performs wonders that cannot be fathomed,
miracles that cannot be counted."
–Job 5:9

When we stop to wonder, we stop to worship.

Part 1

Touched by God

A personal account of the miraculous healing of my daughter
Shasha

Shasha as a young girl in Iloilo City, 1986

THE FIRST DOCUMENT

Dear Reader:

Please consider this to be the product of my natural urge to communicate.

What I am going to share with you is a factual account of what happened to my family within a period of *one week*. This proved to be the longest week we have so far experienced in our lives. It began on November 8, 1991.

Today is November 16, 1991.

Presently, I am 42 years old. I can say that this event is still in progress as I write this, and has definitely caused tremendous changes in my old perception about who I am and where I am going.

My wife, Mariquit, and I have been married for 18 years. Our 5 children, namely, Claudine Marie (17), Roland Lester (16), Melody (15), Credence (14), and Rolando, Jr. (13), are all in school.

I will touch on the otherwise strange, but highly inspiring story about our third child, Melody (nicknamed Shasha). Perhaps, you've heard stories similar to this earlier. And, you might have expressed disbelief as your natural response to such stories.

If so, I can assure you that we come from the same mold.

Today, however, I hold the privilege of suspending disbelief. The chronicle of events that you are about to read actually happened. As a parent, I assume the role of an active participant in this narrative – the author who can write with authority about occurrences unraveling before my eyes.

I stand witness to a miracle that brought me down to the area of simple and straightforward faith—faith in someone whom you could not see, faith in something which you could not touch or understand.

For whatever personal reaction you may have later, please feel free to get in touch with me. Otherwise, please leave all things to God.

November 16, 1991

18

PRELUDE

At Colegio de la Purisima Concepcion in Roxas City as a 3rd year High School student, Shasha had fainted in school a dozen times within a year.

Her mother and I had to fetch her from the school's clinic and rush her to St. Anthony's Hospital for medical and laboratory tests every time this happened.

She was consistently found to be anemic (low in hemoglobin). We attributed this to her improper eating habit. She stubbornly held on to her program of losing weight by skipping meals, supper the previous night and breakfast the following morning.

During her last fainting spell a month ago, she began complaining of severe headache. We had her take Biogesic tablets and Iron supplements, even as Dr. Elfego Londres was consulted who prescribed Flanax.

Her headache persisted. Dr. Londres referred her to Dr. Rex Decolongon, a neurologist at Capiz Emmanuel Hospital on October 17, 1991.

Tentatively, Dr. Decolongon observed that Shasha could be experiencing the early symptoms of epilepsy. Actually, I had an uncle who was epileptic and who died at a young age four years before.

Since the diagnosis was far from conclusive, she was advised to undergo EEG test at the Iloilo Doctors Hospital in Iloilo City the following day, October 18.

She showed abnormal tracings in the strobe light testing. She was advised by Dr. Epifania Sobrevega, also a neurologist in Iloilo City, to refrain from going to discotheques and to minimize playing with TV computers.

The constant headache was by then aggravated by the feeling of heaviness on the top of her head. There seemed to be some amount of water deposited in that area, and she had to prop her head up with her hand while walking around.

Her condition was getting worse. It was at this point that we sought additional attention from a neuro-psychologist, who just happened to be the husband of Dr. Sobrevega. That was on October 26, in Roxas City. A second consultation was on October 29, in Iloilo City.

Shasha was given oral medication to relieve her of the pain and regain her appetite for food and sleep. Yet, the feeling of heaviness in her head persisted. She had to lie down most of the time, as she began missing her classes in school.

She could now only eat a little, was very irritable and never did we see her smile at anyone of us during that period. She was the exact opposite of her former bright and carefree self.

Succeeding tests by Dr. Decolongon and Dr. Sobrevega would give normal impressions, but the burden of heaviness on her head would not leave her. They both recommended a computerized brain scan procedure in Iloilo City.

NOVEMBER 8, 1991

THE ENEMY WITHIN

Our longest week started on November 8, 1991 (Friday). The computerized brain scanning was conducted by Dr. Adah Grace Catedral of Iloilo Doctors Hospital. It was a highly tense and heart-breaking moment when we were informed about the unwelcome results of the test.

Shasha was diagnosed to be suffering from communicating hydrocephalus. Fluid is collecting inside her head, but doesn't drain out via the spinal column. This caused the brain to be pushed against the skull resulting in the feeling of heaviness, severe pain, and Shasha's irritability.

The solution to the problem was surgery which was beyond what Dr. Sobrevega could do at that moment. He, therefore, referred us to a noted neurosurgeon, Dr. Rolando Padilla.

We managed to see Dr. Padilla at nearly 5:00 p.m., who was supposed to be out of his clinic at that time, as otherwise we were set to travel back to Roxas City in an uncertain and dark-night driving.

Dr. Padilla made sketches of the surgical procedure. A shunt made of plastic tube with delicate mechanism, will be implanted in the brain and sewn down to the stomach area for the fluid to drain. There was no other option as medication alone could not correct the problem.

Shasha's official brain scan results from November 8, 1991

It is supposed to be a "simple" kind of surgery lasting for at least 2 hours. The patient can be good again after about ten days.

The shunt will be removed later at such a time when the brain is found to expel its excess fluid normally again.

It was recommended that the operation must be done within ten days' time.

Shasha was a beautiful but broken young girl as we silently filed out of Dr. Padilla's clinic. She couldn't finally hold herself. She broke down and cried out her fears about what might happen to her. She resisted the idea of anybody opening up her head.

I had to pull her close to me as we walked. I wanted to protect her. We reassured her about the bright prospects for her recovery. We made her believe that things would work out well.

We kept her strong all the way. Yet, I was terribly broken inside my hard outer shell. We were fighting something and we were determined to lick the intruder. But, the actual combat was to be fought by people not quite known to us, in the cold arena of the surgical room.

I felt helpless, just like what my daughter must have felt at the moment. Only much worse for her.

THE BATTLE WITHIN

As we reached home after a long 2-hour drive, we decided that the operation must be done immediately. We agreed along the way to return to Iloilo City on Monday afternoon (November 11), and schedule the surgery on the following day.

A few people, friends especially, would tell me sometimes that I am a "good guy". Definitely, however, nobody can ever accuse me of being a religious guy.

I wanted to put meaning to my religion. At that point, I had too many unresolved questions regarding religious beliefs and church doctrines. I was baptized three times in three different faiths, and that left me even more confused.

I was telling a friend, Ray Quijano, one day, "Ray, we should be envious of simple and ignorant folks who put in hundred percent of their faith in their chosen religions. They are so sure of their salvation and nothing could bother them anymore. Look at us. We ask too many questions and we remain lost."

For many years, I've heard about people who found God while they were in their worst human conditions. Hardened criminals sometimes experienced spiritual conversion while serving their term behind bars. Defeated individuals often manage to stretch out their arms to God because they have nowhere else to go but up.

I was then prompted to ask: Is it indeed necessary for man to be wounded for him to experience spiritual healing?

NOVEMBER 10, 1991

Before going any further, let me provide you with some background information on one lady named Mrs. Hilda (Nena) D. Ong.

Who is Nena Ong? Vic and his wife, Nena Ong, are into a highly extensive operation of a 137 hectareage of fishponds dedicated to prawn culturing in Capiz Province, for the export market. They also happen to be our leading performers in our Roxas District Office of Insular Life. I hold the responsibilities of the District Manager as we engage in marketing life insurance products and manpower development.

Their daughter, Hyacinth (Hya), is now a second-year Commerce student at the University of the Philippines in Iloilo. At the age of 17 in 1990, Hya suffered from a disease diagnosed by her doctors merely as "creeping allergy" in her internal organs. She lost a kidney which was later found to be a good one, and almost had one of her ureters and another kidney taken out, too.

Despite advanced medication in Manila, the onslaught of the disease could not be stemmed. The infection was spreading and her doctors in Makati Medical Center, where she was confined, have referred her to UCLA in California, USA, merely to be treated as research material. No amount of money was spared to pay off bills for her to get back to health. The hospital room she was confined in was the same room used by former Philippine President Ferdinand E. Marcos while being treated for his ailments during the closing years of his dictatorial rule.

It was at this desperate hour that Nena came across healing by prayers.

Through prayers alone, Hya was pulled back to life after a month from sure death. All kinds of medication were stopped as the prayer therapy began. Only Faith in God's power to make all things possible was applied.

The prescription of unquestioning faith pointed unerringly to the miraculous cure. Presently, Nena assumes some kind of an inspiration to administer healing work, free of charge. Only a premium on faith is required in the healing powers of God.

This Sunday afternoon, I was attending to our little store when Shasha arrived onboard a tricycle from the house. She was propping her head with her left hand on her way to attend the 4:00 p.m. mass at the cathedral.

It was only 3:00 p.m. and too early for church. So, I just again opened to Shasha my suggestion to go to Nena Ong's residence, which she turned down twice in the past.

This time she resisted again somewhat, but I persuaded her to come on the pretext that we shall merely be paying a courtesy visit to Nena prior to our trip to Iloilo City for the surgery on the following day.

When we arrived, Nena had her hands full. She was interpreting oral messages communicated by divine sources through a lady-instrument named Majeline (nicknamed Maj), who is actually the nursemaid of Nena's youngest 5-year old child, Daphne.

Shasha, as usual, was holding her head up with her right hand when it was her turn to be blessed. I was squatting directly behind her for support in case she drops off on the floor out of sheer exhaustion.

THE HEALING BEGINS

The first message for Shasha contained a promise, saying in part, "Continue to hold faith in Us because no disease is incurable. Nothing is impossible with God." This message came from the Virgin Mary.

Shasha missed the 4:00 p.m. mass. Instead, we were able to attend the 5:30 p.m. mass at Mt. Carmel Church, together with my wife who was greatly surprised by my invitation (of all people!) to go.

For the first time, I felt something new stirring within me as I started to consider the life-and-death meaning of going to church as part of my daughter's therapy.

The instruction was to dedicate three days of "vigil" while offering prayers for Shasha's recovery every hour from morning to midnight, consisting of the "I Believe", "Our Father", "Hail Mary", and "Glory Be", repeated three times with special intentions.

I could not memorize any one of the required prayers. So, I had to read from the pamphlet. I had to totally soak my whole self in the new-found meaning of these prayers. Anointing of the Holy Water follows the hourly vigil.

After supper at home, we returned to Nena Ong's residence to embark on a program of bombarding heaven with our prayers.

Shasha was told to kneel down and light the altar candle before we began praying. It was a pitiful sight as Shasha tried to gather her strength to light the candle with a match, but could not do it. Her arms were weak and her hands were shaking while she could hardly kneel down firmly on the floor. She was physically drained. Somebody else had to light the candle up for her.

As we were preparing to arrange ourselves inside the prayer room, I was struck by the sweet scent of roses filling my nose.

I looked at the altar which contained two small vases of white flowers looking like carnation, but there was not a single rose there. I kissed Daphne's hair who was sitting down close to me, but it faintly smelled of freshly-washed shampoo. Yet, the smell of roses persisted.

Showing and feeling no alarm over this phenomenon, I innocently announced that I smelled the fragrance of flowers. Quickly, other people inside the room remarked with astonishment that they too smelled it. Shasha who was in front of the altar said that she smelled the fragrance also.

The message from the Virgin Mary during our first-hour prayer was re-assuring. She spoke about interceding to God the Father and the Son on behalf of Shasha. In part She said, "... fight off your illness. Continue to have faith in Us, and you will be cured."

There was an immediate and perceptible change in Shasha that was beginning to show. She was now kneeling straight and regaining her strength after the *third* hourly prayer.

To our great relief and surprise, she was now the one who lighted up the candle without much effort as we prepared to begin with our fourth-hour prayers. We were all encouraged, but still watchful about being too optimistic.

While on our way home that night, the pervading scent of roses filled our car we were riding on. When we reached home, our living room was awash with the fragrance of roses as we were preparing to say our 11:00 p.m. prayers.

Claudine, our eldest child, felt faint and light-headed out of fear inside the bedroom she shares with Shasha. She kept on smelling fresh roses inside the room while they were preparing to go to sleep.

I remember that it was Shasha who announced first about the scent of roses that seemed to emanate immediately around her.

Promptly, I decided to withdraw all kinds of medication starting that evening and leave the healing to God.

NOVEMBER 11, 1991

Monday dawned with hope in our hearts. We all felt groggy from lack of sleep. Our bags were packed ready as we prepared to depart for Iloilo City after lunch for the surgery.

Shasha requested that we should visit her school to ask permission to be absent and bid goodbye to her teachers and classmates, and ask for prayers as well. The school Principal, Fr. Clemente Fungot, asked us to advise them about the day and time of the surgery so that they could be alerted to offer their prayer as a group.

However, we decided to see Nena Ong again after our visit to the school, and finally agreed to cancel our trip to Iloilo City.

The vigil resumed that morning. Additional change was observed as Shasha began to disengage her hand from propping her head.

The feeling of heaviness in her head had left her. She began to talk in her usual lively manner and she was her high-spirited self again. Could something truly wonderful really be happening?

That afternoon, fifteen of Shasha's classmates paid her a visit. A sorry episode took place as Maj tried to resist her positive vibrations in deference to an assembly of strangers inside the prayer room.

That session left Shasha feeling weak, drained and sleepy. She succumbed to sleep even before her visitors had left.

She quickly regained her strength after the following hourly vigil as the message that came from the Virgin Mary exhorted us to banish our doubts, and asked the whole family for prayers.

NOVEMBER 12, 1991

Tuesday was the significant turning point. Shasha visibly showed her original zest and love for life. She woke up in a cheerful manner and in high spirits that morning, and she did not complain about anything at all.

Nena was quite positive that Shasha's complete recovery had been achieved in less than forty-eight hours. This record is impressive given the gravity of her illness.

Something strange occurred at about 11:00 a.m. that day. While Shasha was lying asleep on a foam mattress on the prayer room floor, she slowly assumed the position of the Miraculous Virgin. She stretched her legs straight out and spread her arms apart, half-way up by her left and right sides.

My wife and I failed to witness this phenomenon because I stayed back in the office that morning. She too went back to work. We were so assured that our daughter was in good and caring hands.

We were told about it only when we visited her at lunch-time and found her eating like a normally hungry and growing teen-ager. Her appetite had definitely returned.

As told by Shasha, while deep in sleep she had her first vision of herself with the Virgin Mary poised to climb a heavenly ladder made of gold. The ladder was less than two meters wide with hand-support on its left side, and running all the way up to a point where the steps meet the sky.

The Lady was urging her to step on the ladder but she was overwhelmed by her feeling of doubt and uncertainty about this new experience. She was feeling afraid, but she won over her fear when the Lady told her to spread out her arms everytime she felt afraid.

It was supposedly at this moment when Shasha felt a force that moved her arms and legs involuntarily in a rigid position while asleep.

Her feet felt heavy as she made her first step up the golden ladder. To her surprise, the Lady floated up along with her while holding Shasha on her right shoulder to guide her.

Shasha managed to ask the Lady if she would be cured of her illness, to which the Lady answered, "Yes."

"Am I going to die?" Shasha asked again,

"No, not now, "the Lady replied, "but, at the appointed time when you will be called."

Upon reaching the top of the long flight of stairs, Shasha saw the presence of God behind a film of white haze. A bank of clouds separated them. The man-figure was seated on a chair of gold, and Shasha could discern His white beard.

He spoke to her, "You will be called if We see no change in your father, mother and your family." It was a Fatherly message simply delivered and quickly understood by a young child. Shasha stood transfixed with her head bowed in awe and submission.

In attendance were angels of all ages surrounding the Father and singing a heavenly song. Shasha could distinctly hear the word "Alleluia!" repeatedly sung by the angels. The heavens fell silent when the Father begun to speak.

After her encounter with the Father, Shasha floated down with the Lady as the angelic choir continued to sing "Alleluia!" The Lady told Shasha, "Child, you may now wake up."

At this point, the Lady drew back with a trace of a smile on her face. Shasha slowly moved her arms back ever so smoothly, hands clasped on top of her abdomen and she returned to soft wakefulness as her whole body began to relax.

This first episode of her trance started and ended with Shasha expelling air by yawning audibly, the way all subsequent episodes would go.

Shasha woke up totally disoriented as she stretched her body like one who wakes up revived in the morning. She somehow liked the feeling of being "there", and regretted returning to her conscious level.

A FLOOD OF VISIONS

The second trance occurred early that afternoon. My wife and I were present to witness it. Shasha announced that another trance was coming on. She felt the back portion of her neck grow heavy and the overpowering urge to close her eyes to sleep took over.

Here's her account: The beautiful Lady who is garbed in white underneath a blue robe, is back. Shasha was not as timid this time since her familiarity with the Lady had developed.

Like any young girl who is curious about where she is, she asked the Lady if she could explore the place with Her.

The Lady smiled warmly as she beckoned at her to come. Shasha was brought to a beautiful garden full of flowers, mostly roses, not unlike flower gardens one could see back on earth.

Shasha saw mostly red-colored roses in that garden. They moved through the garden together. There she saw a number of angels (human-like figures with wings) lulling in the area individually or in groups, who greeted them brightly with smiles.

Shasha felt welcomed. She was able to touch particularly red roses as the Lady guided her around with Her hand on Shasha's shoulder most of the time. Moments passed and it was time to part again.

When Shasha woke up, her fingers actually smelled of the fragrance of the roses she touched during her tour of the garden.

I can testify without reservation to the truth of everything that I am telling you now. I am a living and first-hand witness to these occurrences.

On our way home at about 6:30 pm, my wife and I decided to drop by Mt. Carmel Church for confession (my first), with the guidance of an office associate and close friend, Jun Abella.

Fr. Abalajon, whom we met for the first time, was the only priest available to hear our unscheduled confessions. I was the last to confess. Shasha went into another trance in the convent's receiving room while alone with her mother, since Jun Abella went out for a smoke.

Her mother was unsure about what to do as she saw her daughter's face light up with a smile; Shasha was smiling brightly as her mother watched her closely with great alarm. Our daughter was actually having a vision of the Virgin Mary who was a picture of happiness.

The episode ended precisely at the time when Jun Abella returned to the room. He never had any idea what took place until he was told about it.

THE MESSAGES

At home that night, Shasha experienced yet another trance where she began a relaxed conversation with the Lady. While Shasha was having her trances, all of us would kneel down in prayer.

Messages she brought to us that night were the following:

1. For Jun Abella who wanted to stop smoking, but could not, "Call on Us for help. Do not lose your faith in Us."

2. To Shasha for her brothers and sister, "Tell them to help you pray."

3. For our youngest son (Junjun) who was seen by Shasha's classmates praying in church for her that morning, "He is a good boy. He can help you much because We are listening to his prayers."

4. For me, "Your father is a good man. May he continue to hold his faith in Us because We are ready to help him."

5. For Shasha, "I will watch over you wherever you are. May your faith in Us last for your lifetime until We will finally call you."

6. For Shasha's brothers and sister, "Help pray for your beloved sister so that she can serve you and Us. Banish your doubts because with Us nothing is impossible."

A second trance that night had the following messages from the Virgin Mary:

1. To Junjun who complained of having a headache, "Rest and you'll be healed by your faith in Us." (He was well the following morning.)

2. For me who couldn't find the plastic hook for the front sunscreen of our Lancer car, "It's just inside your car. Don't worry, you'll find it. Trust in Us." (I found it instantly as if it was merely lying in wait for me on the floor when I opened the car to clean it up the following morning.)

3. For my wife, "Have faith in Us, We are helping you. Keep on praying while invoking the name of the Father, the Son and the Holy Spirit. We are just beside you together with your child. Believe in what she says."

NOVEMBER 13, 1991

Shasha is experiencing frequent visits from the Virgin Mary even now. They seem to be carrying on the relationship of new-found friends with one frequently calling on the other for visits.

She is having several trances a day. Special messages expressing concern for her mother kept coming, as follows:

1. "My child, you can do much for your mother. Hold on to your faith. I will protect you."

2. "My child, help your mother and those people who need your help. Keep calling on Us and We will be here for you. Believe in the Father, the Son and the Holy Spirit.

NOVEMBER 14, 1991

W e scheduled our trip back today to Iloilo City. We were determined to verify the results of a second brain scan in less than a week, not merely to put to rest whatever doubts we had regarding Shasha's miraculous healing, but also other people's doubts.

I was fully convinced that my daughter was completely healed the previous day, Wednesday. It would require a documented evidence to make other people believe this and reinforce their faith in the Divine Healer.

So, I went by car with my wife, Shasha and our youngest child, Junjun. We brought Junjun along, equipped with his prayers memorized by heart, with pen and paper ready for the messages that may come along as we drove to the city.

While cruising the highway, Shasha had a trance inside the car. As recorded by Junjun, the following messages were given:

1. To my wife, "Keep calling on Us. You alone can help yourself. Come near Us, especially to the Father."

2. For us in the car, "Don't be afraid as you travel because I am here to protect you."

3. To Shasha, "My child, help your mother. Call on Us and We will help you. Trust on the Father, the Son and the Holy Spirit."

4. To Shasha, "We are happy about your father because he accepted. Tell him not to be afraid because you are there to help them in the name of the Father, the Son and the Holy Spirit. Have faith and I will be there to protect you for your whole lifetime. You were chosen to help the people who will come to you for help. Remember my words. I am here just beside you."

Minutes after the trance, Shasha began to sing very sweetly a familiar song I often heard being sung in church during the offertory. (I found later the title of the song to be "Tanging Yaman", loosely translated as My Only Treasure.) I failed to hold my tears back. I cried in a manner I never cried before.

I stopped the car along a curve in a mountainside and cried my heart out at the thought that I would not be listening to my daughter singing then had the surgery gone on as planned. It was an act of crying that washed away all pains.

When we reached Iloilo City, we went directly to Iloilo Doctors Hospital. Dr. Padilla wouldn't allow Shasha to undergo a second brain scan at this time (a brain scan costs us P4,800.00, or $110 in today's rate of exchange).

He initially evaluated, however, that Shasha's condition was getting worse especially when she fell into a trance in his presence while sitting down on the patient's chair. The Lady was reassuring her that she was healed.

Shasha also fell thrice into a trance inside the CT scan room, triggered perhaps by her feeling of anxiety upon seeing the scanning machine used a week ago to diagnose her illness. The male technician, a Mr. Gustilo, and two nurses who were stationed in this area detected the scent of roses inside the room and they reacted with much wonder and surprise.

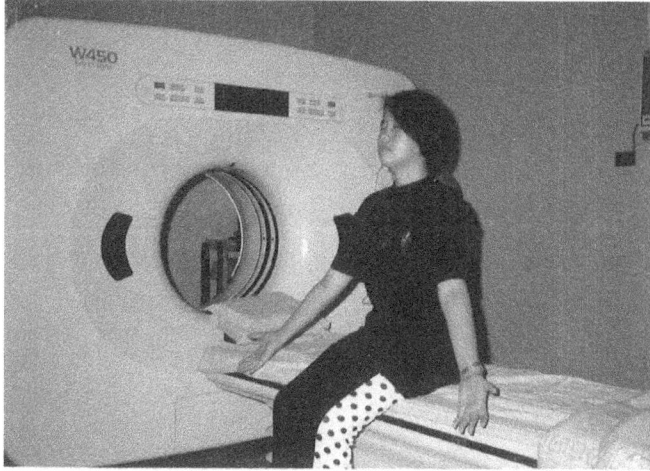

The scent of roses filled the CT Scan Room of Iloilo Doctors Hospital in Iloilo City, when Shasha fell into a trance.

Dr. Padilla conducted routine tests and indicated that Shasha was showing normal signs after all. Another brain scan may be scheduled two months later.

One thing confused me. Dr. Padilla revealed that he had conferred with Dr. Sobrevega about the brain scan results. Both could not determine conclusively what caused Shasha's hydrocephalus.

Generally, hydrocephalus can be traced to an infection or a tumor, neither of which applies in this case. As we drove home that afternoon, we were awed by the thought about something which developed through an unexplained cause, and responded positively to an equally unexplainable method of cure.

A TEST OF FAITH

While resting early in bed that night, my wife confided in me that one of the nurses at Iloilo Doctors who sneaked into the CT scan room to witness Shasha's falling into a trance, observed her rapid eye movement.

She was told to keep a close watch because this usually points to a clear symptom that a patient of hydrocephalus could go blind in due time.

This prognosis invariably planted another healthy seed of doubt in my heart because I had actually observed the same. Although we tried hard to reassure ourselves, I could not prevent my elbows from turning to jelly as we discussed the uncertain turn of events.

The nightmare of seeing my daughter become blind and sitting uselessly in a corner was very hard to me. May God not allow this to happen.

After supper, I asked Shasha to pray with us in bed. In the middle of our prayers, she felt sleepy once more as she showed signs of another trance coming.

In a short while she was on her back in bed in the position of the Miraculous Virgin. This gave us the opportunity to watch intently her closed eyelids in particular.

Wonder of wonders! We felt relieved to observe that her eyes **did not** move at all until she woke up.

We were even more shocked in silence to listen to her blurt out these words immediately after she regained her strength, "Daddy, from now on my eyes will not move again while I am in a trance."

Caught by surprise and truly amazed, my wife and I merely looked at each other properly chastised. Must we still doubt?

Shasha never knew about the question tormenting us but she had unwittingly provided the answer straightaway without delay, and in no uncertain terms.

I should note here that this manner of providing answers to our confidential questions regarding Shasha's condition happened a few more times. Questions asked mentally are answered orally while she is in a deep trance.

Truly, something outside of the parameters of what we consider as our normal human limits is at work. I make no mistake about it.

NOVEMBER 15, 1991

Tonight, at around 8:00 p.m., Shasha mentioned to me about her blurring vision while the two of us were watching a TV program. I tried to conceal my concern as I told her to ask the Virgin Mary about what to do.

At exactly 8:15 p.m., I had to switch off the TV as the answer came through another trance.

The Lady said, "Close your eyes and lightly rub them with Holy Water and they will be cured. After you wake up in the morning, anoint your body with Holy Water while invoking the name of the Father, the Son and the Holy Spirit. We are here, trust in Us and We will protect you."

So, it was done. And so, again, she was healed.

NOVEMBER 16, 1991

I can record only brief incidents happening at home now as they happen when I am present. It must be noted that Shasha stayed at Nena Ong's residence during the day because she had to be left at home without a companion when we all leave for our offices, school, or the store.

Her falling into a trance had become a regular occurrence although there was no fixed pattern as to when it would happen, how long, or how often.

It was at about 7:15 a.m. when she was again exhorted to: "Help your mother. Call on Us and We will help you heal other people who are sick."

Persistent messages touching on her mother are being communicated even up to this writing. My wife is still being advised to cast away her doubts.

Likewise, having obtained this blessing from God, Shasha eagerly expressed her desire to become an instrument of healing herself. Subsequent messages, therefore, encouraged her to help those who would come to her asking for help.

In one of her visions, she beheld the Virgin Mary with her outstretched palms radiating with light. Shasha was made to cover her own right palm over the radiating right palm of the Miraculous Virgin and that bestowed on her the gift of healing.

A GLIMPSE OF HEAVEN

Early that evening, precocious as she was, Shasha ventured to ask the Virgin Mary during a trance, if she could take a further look of her surroundings. The Lady flashed an amused smile and beckoned at her to come.

At that point, Shasha was observed to be enjoying herself as she giggled a lot. Daphne, Mrs. Ong's 5-year old daughter, was giggling along with her and immensely enjoying the scene as she was slumped beside Shasha who was laughing convulsively a few times.

As reported by Shasha, the experience brought her to a place where she saw animals in their natural habitat that looked like the earth itself. There were adult monkeys scratching their heads and making faces at her while the little ones romped around.

She saw lions lounging peacefully in the grass with elephants and giraffes. She saw dolphins in aerial show in a pool in pairs. What particularly made her laugh were baby crocodiles idling on a river with their parents.

A half-dozen baby crocodiles were enjoying the water as Shasha attempted to stretch her hand down to touch them. The baby crocodiles made an attempt to snap at her hand which she jerked out of the water.

She did this several times which made her giggle and laugh a lot. One of the adult crocodiles opened its mouth to react, but was glued motionless when the Lady looked at it warningly.

It was at that time when she finally found the answer to my long-standing question of whether there are fruits to be eaten there, too. Indeed, there were. She saw a grapevine heavy with fruit. She picked one and ate it. She said it tasted quite delicious!

The experience was like being in the company of animals in some special place on earth, except that everything happened while she was too far beyond earthly realities. In her words, "Earth looks like heaven, except for some slight deviations."

The Lady gave her the reassurance of extending Her mantle of protection to her during her healing activity. She was also told to pray for her mother.

THE DAYS AFTER

We managed through the week, which proved to be the longest week I had ever experienced in my life. Shasha's illness (and miraculous healing) opened many doors for me as a person. I am seeing life much differently now than before.

At about 1:00 p.m. at Vic and Nena Ong's residence, we were waiting for the healing session to begin. A full week after Shasha was diagnosed to be seriously ill, she was getting ready to become an instrument of healing herself on account of an undisguised miracle.

That was when she conducted her first healing service, and for the first time we witnessed how unclean spirits would attempt to mislead.

November 17, 1991

After long days of absence, Shasha was returning to school. She experienced several trances even while classes were in session. One of her female classmates, Remy Adepin, fainted perhaps because of anxiety.

Shasha revived Remy by praying over her. She asked for plain water, prayed over it, and used it to anoint Remy's forehead. The girl regained consciousness amid the cheers of her classmates and her astonished teacher, Miss Lolita Marte.

November 18, 1991

Shasha had been complaining about a bad headache since we arrived from Culasi, Antique (a 4-hour drive away) the previous day, where we were visiting my 81-year old mother.

In the afternoon, she came into the office after her classes and she could hardly conceal her feeling of discomfiture. She was having a nasty headache and she was again complaining about her deteriorating eyesight. I began to get worried about her condition once again.

I decided to return to Nena Ong's prayer room in the evening. Once again, we witnessed something very unusual.

While Shasha was lying down on the floor in a trance, the Miraculous Virgin declared her power to free Shasha from what ails her.

Her bent but rigid right arm moved slowly and directed her vibrating hand to the top of her head, and firmly massaged that area ever so lightly down to her forehead.

After remaining on her forehead for a few seconds, her right hand moved to touch her closed eyes in the same manner. All the while, Shasha had been maintaining a serene facial expression while deep in sleep. Her hand simply kept on vibrating with an unseen energy over her eyes and head.

This procedure was repeated three times, which lasted for not more than five minutes. At the end, the healing arm motioned to bless her whole body to signal the conclusion of the healing process.

Upon waking up, Shasha announced that she was healed. Her headache left her without a trace. She looked truly refreshed, revived and glowing. She was told she was merely tired after our long journey to Antique during the weekend. It was a unique episode we witnessed, about a healer who healed herself.

As witnesses, we have no reason to doubt her words. Instead, they helped to reaffirm our faith in **Someone** and **Something** truly mysterious and wonderful.

I can bear witness to things that are now happening whose *why's* and *how's* hold no clear answers to satisfy our quest for wisdom and understanding. I have, henceforth, stopped to question those that are beyond my human mind's capacity to comprehend.

As you read through this account, please be guided by what best you should do on the strength of **FAITH** alone. Meanwhile, this strange but highly inspiring story continues.

God bless us all.

November 25, 1991

BLESSED RETURNS

It is now nearly thirteen years after this life-changing experience. All our five children are now married. We are blessed with seven grandchildren to date. Shasha herself has a 2-year old son whom she left with us while she went to visit her brothers in California: Lester and Junjun. Claudine lives in Roxas City; Credence in Iloilo City.

It must be noted that Shasha never had any recurrence of her ailment since she was healed. Her healing has been permanent.

She wasn't able to devote her life to a ministry of healing, but we are forever thankful to God for His enduring love.

We are in contact with Mrs. Nena Ong, whose family is now deeply involved in the service of God and man.

The Lord has been so good to everyone. Rejoice, because HE truly lives!

May 23, 2004

A week after Shasha's (third from the right) miraculous healing, with some friends

Shasha and her 8-month old daughter, Jeanne Rose
June 2010

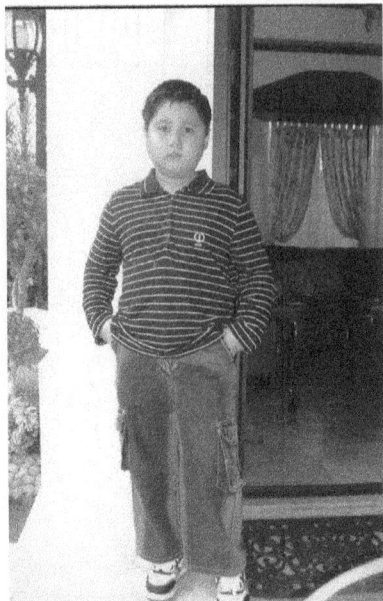

8 year old John Andrey, the
older of Shasha's two kids
May 2010

"O Lord my God, You have made Your servant king instead of my father David, but I am a little child; I do not know how to go out or come in."

-1 KINGS 3:7

Part 2

Faith, Perseverance, and Transformation

A personal account of the 18 years following my daughter's miraculous healing

PICKING UP THE THREAD

TODAY is 04 September 2010, Saturday. This day stands as some sort of watermark for my personal account about the miraculous healing of my daughter, Shasha, which I put down on paper on 16 November 1991. It is *18 years and 10 months* since I wrote that testimony.

For some people, 18 years could mean a complete, but brief, stretch of one lifetime spent on this earth. For a few others past their gold-year mark, 18 years is one big stride in this grand marathon of life. For me, however, the past 18 years served as the Litmus Test to affirm the validity of a *living miracle* my family went through within a period of one week (8-15 Nov 1991). It earned a permanent place in my heart and changed my life forever.

My previous writings have been used as a tool for countless others to strengthen their faith in God. It earned scoffs from some. *Was it all a trick of the devil, or a real miracle from God?* Over time I learned that I could not anticipate how people would react after reading my account. Somehow, this gave me the wisdom to understand some texts I've read in the Book of Matthew on why Jesus admonished some people He healed not to tell the others about what had just happened to them.

After restoring the leper in Matthew 8:4, Jesus said, *"See that you don't tell anyone."* In Matthew 9:29, after healing the blind and the mute, Jesus warned them by saying, *"See that no one knows about this."* I'd been asking myself then, **why** *"don't tell anyone"*? Certainly, Jesus' words of caution fall within the context of instant healings He performed as supplementary to God's Great Plan for Man. Jesus' miraculous healing of the sick was part of His mission, but not its core. Jesus knew about the human tendency to put even good motives under question. Matthew 9:34 holds part of the answer to my "why" question, in the way the Pharisees reacted to Jesus' miracles. They concluded that, *"It* *is by the prince of demons that he (Jesus) drives out demons."* Jesus could have been the most misunderstood man during His brief time spent on earth.

Reproduced copies of my testimony reached innumerable people in many areas. The story helped greatly in starting a healing movement known today as the *Holy Trinity Divine Healing Ministry.* It emanated from the exact place where the miraculous healing of my daughter took place—the Ong Residence in Dayao, Roxas City, Province of Capiz, the Philippines.

TRANSITION AND TRANSFORMATION

Earth-time consists of the regular cycle of sunrises and sunsets occurring without fail on a fixed seasonal pattern. We wish to feel good as we continue to live in harmony with the laws of nature. Along the way, man goes through various stages of personal triumphs (represented by the sunny days) and failures (defined by the shimmering shades of night) in his lifetime. We are all objects moving in step with the ebb and flow of life.

After basking under the blinding light of the sun for weeks, the time finally came when my family and I had to face the onset of the darkening night which came without warning and without any possibility for escape. How would you have responded to the unusual phenomenon of the sun failing to show up at sunrise one day?

Upon reflection, it has become clear to me that the miraculous healing of my daughter 18 years ago, actually meant two things for us:

1. It led to the miraculous physical healing of my daughter, and

2. It resulted in the re-direction of my personal walk into the realm of the spiritual in that precise period of my life. *Not a heartbeat late, nor a breath too soon!*

THE NIGHT ADVENT

My wife and I have been together for thirty-seven years now. We plunged into married life on 30 April 1973 in San Jose, Antique. She was only 23 then, I was 24.

She worked in a government office, and I was employed with a life insurance firm. Our five children subsequently came one after the other almost on a yearly basis. We opted to transfer our work venue and residence to Iloilo City in 1974. We functioned excellently as a team, obsessed with our desire to bring our children up as best we could through hard work.

In 1989, I accepted the offer of being assigned to Roxas City for supervisory tasks. That started the series of promotions I earned for a job well done. My wife, at about the same time, obtained a one-year US Tourist Visa. She left for New York to work for eleven months there, and left me alone with the children who were all in their elementary grade school levels.

Back in 1978, I got a loan from my employer to purchase a house and lot in Lapaz, Iloilo City, payable in 20 years through monthly salary deductions. I was then only 29. It wasn't long before I finally owned a car and acquired many things usually coveted by young professionals on the rise. I felt I was invincible. I could have everything I fancied simply by working hard and being smart. During those days, the relevance of God in the work place was not part of my self-designed formula for my personal advancement.

There were moments, however, when I was searching and thirsting for God. While my wife was out of the country, I would go out of the house alone in the evenings, and look up at the sky filled with twinkling little stars, to search for the face of God: *"Where are you, Lord? Please give me a little sign about Your presence among the stars so I'll know that You are real."* I would wait and wait for a sign. I felt ignored by His non-response. I was losing grip.

I was baptized in a non-Catholic church when I was a child. My family was converted to a Protestant faith when I was 15 years old, and I had my second baptism. I was baptized, for the third time, as a Catholic to meet the requirement of getting married in church. Such mix-up in my religious orientation left me confused and questioning: *Why can't the Christian religion be one?* I was looking for the answer among the stars. I found none. *It could be somewhere else?*

The answer came after a three-year wait from the time of my night vigils among the stars. It was given to me at a moment when I least expected it. It came during my most vulnerable state, when I was desperate about my child's health condition. Certainly, God knows exactly *how, when* and *where* to touch us in granting answers to our prayers. I would like to repeat what I said before: *not a heartbeat late, or a breath too soon!*

He, surely, didn't want me to just see Him far away among the stars in the night sky. If it were so, then, the experience would have been too fleeting and without meaning. He wanted me to offer my heart deep inside my being as His permanent dwelling place where I can be with Him no matter what time of day or night it is! He revealed Himself to me in His own time, and through His own terms. *His timing was perfect!*

We experienced the living presence of God through Shasha's miraculous healing. My ignorance vanished because I stopped to question. I felt I was no longer alone. To me now, total surrender to Him means total freedom – from my doubts, fears and aimlessness. *Finally, I found myself in His reassuring grip.*

Within the 18 years of our lives after my daughter was miraculously healed, my family went through cycles of unprecedented collapse that bordered on our collective deaths and eventual re-births. Through all this, we were made to feel that we were not alone in our journey through life. *Even now.*

EIGHTEEN YEARS AFTER THE FACT

The ensuing weeks after Shasha's complete recovery transported us back into our familiar daily stream of activities: *house, work, school.* Just one new activity was added to the pattern. After church in the morning, Sunday afternoons were dedicated to Shasha's healing mission at Mrs. Ong's residence.

What used to be their garage was re-modeled and converted into a prayer center. The place could now accommodate the growing number of people who sought the healing of their various physical ailments by prayers. News of miraculous healings taking place there spread fast, far and wide.

I was a witness when Shasha prayed for an old woman who was deaf for years. After praying, we were kneeling down as usual while Shasha's right hand was vibrating with energy about an inch away from the woman's head. Suddenly, I saw the woman's right ear drip with some clear liquid which the woman tried to wipe off down her shoulder. Softly, I asked her if she could hear me talking to her. She answered in a clear voice: "Yes, I can hear now!"

On three separate occasions when I was experiencing recurrent headaches which might have been brought about by pressures from my job (I was found later to have a high Cholesterol level), Shasha asked me to sit down on a chair. As she was about to raise her healing arm, I maintained a detached outlook and prevented myself from feeling positive nor negative about what would happen next. I toyed with the idea that God won't be bothered at all by a small guy complaining of an ordinary headache.

Shasha's vibrating right hand passed around my head three times. Slowly, I could feel my head growing light as the dulling ache completely left me. It was as if some magical hand lifted off the burdensome weight off my system in an instant. As I've mentioned, this happened during three separate occasions, which proved that my own personal healing by prayer passed the test even of practical science. They did not happen only by chance. That was an unprecedented 100% success rate to reckon with! Could there be any stain of doubt still on anybody's mind?

Another high point of our family's spiritual odyssey happened in the week after Shasha's healing. It took place at about 6 o'clock in the evening after an early dinner. As we prepared to organize ourselves to pray the Holy Rosary before a makeshift altar in our living room, we were like kids full of excitement as we were set to try our best to know by heart how to pray the Rosary by ourselves.

The evening was cool and quiet. Not a whiff of air from outside or inside the house was evident. So, we kneeled down to pray. We were about to begin praying when, suddenly, we were startled by the banging sound of the boys' bedroom door closing, located just about 8 feet away from us. *BANG!* It happened as if somebody slammed it rudely with brute force. We looked at each other with shock and alarm. It appeared as if some expression of opposition was being conveyed by an invisible entity so determined to stop us from pursuing what we were doing.

Calmly, I motioned for everyone to ignore the disturbance and go ahead with the Rosary. So, we continued praying. But, like a naughty child who felt rebuffed for his mischief, the unseen force didn't lose a minute and went on to bang shut the girls' bedroom door opposite our boys' room. *BANG!* How could the two bedroom doors facing each other directly swing closed with such force on such a quiet and windless night?

We all tried to hide our fright as we stubbornly went on with the Rosary. Finally, we finished the Rosary as beginners would – fumbling, but with a lot of curious stares thrown at each other until the final "Amen". Yes, we did pray the Rosary during that memorable night without further incidents. It became embedded in my mind as another major victory of the spirit for all of us.

No other significant paranormal episodes can be noted from here onwards as everything seemed to have begun to settle down. My life had somewhat returned to normal. I was back to my daily office and home routines again. I had stopped assuming the role of family scribe and historian. I felt then that the chronicle of events I already had on record was completely done. Hence, although I can easily narrate to you today the sequence of events that followed, I cannot provide you with the dates and time *when* they actually happened.

Was my family, on purpose, being prepared to stand fast and fit to face the jarring uncertainties of the coming days through the miraculous healings we experienced? Was the spiritual capital granted to us by God specifically designed to serve as stand-by source of strength during the times of spiritual and moral meltdowns?

Man's purpose on earth of celebrating the sheer mystery of life is usually negated by whatever amount of genius we spend in trying to lay bare life's meaning. Only to fail each time. Yes, that is simply because it's not an issue for the intellect to resolve at any given time during our earthly life. So, we keep on getting confused.

THE DARK IS UPON US

Every morning after waking up, I have not failed to say prayers of gratitude to God for His blessings for the past eighteen years now. It was all so pleasantly different from my old ways. Even at moments when I feel weighed down by domestic and official concerns, saying thanks to God for His gift of life never fails to lift me up. It's *first* in my agenda at waking time. I remember 1 Thessalonians 5:18, *"In everything give thanks."*

The shift in our elements came two months after my daughter's miraculous healing. It came without warning. It caused the quick change in our domestic environment from light to dark. The blast of life-enhancing fresh air has turned overnight into a toxic fume that was extremely suffocating. In a manner of speaking, during that period, the sun failed to show up at sunrise for us.

One quiet morning inside my office, a friend whispered to me something about a big financial problem my wife had been trying to hide from me for months now. Without my knowledge, she engaged in a money-making activity beyond her expertise to manage, with capital borrowed from another friend who charged an interest way above prevailing commercial rates. She dabbled in the Foreign Exchange market and jewelry business with her new-found, seemingly bottomless source of loaned capital.

I was so engrossed with my job. I was doing a self-imposed, back-breaking, 7-day work week then. I would drive out-of-town even on week-ends, developing manpower and widening our market reach. I simply overlooked how I messed up in the home front! My wife kept on drawing borrowed funds in her attempt to stay afloat for a while. All she actually did was to wriggle herself deeper into the sinkhole. Her accountability ran over a million pesos. We were financially ruined overnight. Our net value hit negative in a flash! After staying long under the light, the dark night was spreading then to totally envelop us. We got swallowed far down inside the guts of an unforgiving black hole without warning, without escape.

As if jolted awake from my sleep, I only realized then that I'd been made aware several times beforehand about what to anticipate in that case during the course of my daughter's miraculous healing! I mistook the *earlier messages* to be divine urgings addressed to my wife *alone* on her stance of unbelief. The messages turned out to be admonitions for the family to remain strong in our faith as we moved closer into the eye of the coming storm.

These messages are contained in the following paragraphs of **Part I**:

> For my wife, 'Have faith in Us, We are helping you. Keep on praying while invoking the name of the Father, the Son and the Holy Spirit. We are just beside you and your child. Believe in what she says.'

> 'My child, help your mother and those people who need your help...'

> To my wife, 'Keep calling on Us. You alone can help yourself. Come near Us, especially to the Father.'

> It was at about 7:15am when she was again exhorted: 'Help your mother.'

> Persistent messages touching on her mother are being communicated even up to this writing. My wife is still being advised to cast away her doubts.

As I expressed to my children then, I had mixed feelings for their mother when the sky fell down on us. In terms of emotions quantified, I felt 20% anger and 80% pity for her and our shared pain during those heartbreaking moments. She carried up her heavy load alone without our knowing. She went through the jubilation of our daughter's miraculous healing with a disturbed mind frame.

How shall we manage to go through this wrenching situation with our bodies and souls holding intact? The road ahead looked terrible and menacing. Would even our newly-found faith in God hold fast?

MUSTARD SEED OF FAITH

W e are still human, after all. I felt somebody just snatched the future of our children away from them. We were in shock, disoriented and fearful about what dark forces lurked ahead. All our little savings went into my wife's accountabilities. It was a small drop in a large bucket; it didn't even create a ripple to be of consequence in reducing the account. I carried on the semblance of normalcy before everyone else, but no one had a suspicion that I was in a deep coma.

Along her track, my wife left behind a damning trail of empty checks she issued to a string of people that could convict her, and possibly both of us, in a court of law. Her goal was to take us out on an exciting ride to happiness, but we figured in an explosive flat tire along the way with no spare tire to bring us out of this desolate place. We were in a very complex situation that literally boggled my mind unendingly.

I started having nightmares. I would break into cold sweat in the middle of the night with my chest pounding. *My God, my God! How are we going to find our way out?*

Except for a light game of mahjong with friends on some weekends, I am one who doesn't believe in gambling. One day, I mumbled an urgent prayer to God while buying three Sweepstakes shares from a street vendor, offering a P6 Million windfall. I was praying for another miracle from God, specifically for something worth more than a million pesos in value! Did God listen to me? Did He make me feel He was standing just right beside me as I made my pleadings?

He did listen!

In this desperate hour of need, I saw the block of lottery numbers 174300 jump out of the *Philippine Daily Inquirer* newspaper page, in the draw of 12 January 1992.

I won!

The one and only time ever when I bought a lottery ticket for an urgent purpose, I hit the bull's eye! Regrettably, the amount I won was only a measly sum of **P2,400.00**, at P800.00 per share. It didn't measure up to the moment's need. The jackpot I would soon claim to be mine was not expressed in terms of money value!

The Lord surely passed on the message that He was there with us all along, but doing the lottery was not the best way for me to get us off the hook. God wanted me to grow rich in character, more than He wanted me to strike it rich materially by chance! He seemed to tell me, *"Not the easy way out, smart guy. You can do better than that!"* That gave me a good laugh and momentary respite from my agony. How amused I was!

Now invariably pushed against the wall, I appealed for help from my older sister (*Inday* Zenaida) in America. God was with us when my sister accepted, without hesitation, my offer to sell off to her the house and lot I acquired through a loan from my employer in 1978 (13 years ago). This transaction with my sister provided us with P860,000 to pay off a big part of my wife's accounts.

I felt a tinge of hurt when I made the move to let go of our property. It meant 20 years of hard work going down the drain. What I considered to be one of my major achievements in life, quickly vanished without reason or rhyme. I was stripped of my only shelter and left exposed to the elements while riding out the catastrophic force of the raging storm. I was literally tested on how deeply attached I was to my material possessions. Up to what point would I finally give up and break apart? Thank God, I grew almost immune to pain as I refused to crack under pressure. We had become instantly homeless, with no permanent address to our name any longer! *But, life must go on.*

Meanwhile, it was my company's internal policy to send sales personnel like me on out of town postings for up to a maximum of five years in one place, together with their families. It has been our Management's prerogative to shorten that period of residency for varying reasons, such as one being transferred to a larger territory on account of a promotion in rank.

This was what happened to me when I was given a one-step promotion to Assistant Manager rank in early 1992. The accompanying marching order was for me to assume a new posting in the sugar-rich province of Negros Occidental within the region. This area is considerably larger than Roxas District where I was currently assigned, popularly known to be the seafood capital of the Philippines.

My four-year work assignment in Roxas City (1988-1992), was a bitter-sweet period of advancing professionally and spiritually with my team. From the loving partnership with my staff and marketing team, I earned a couple of promotions in rank for our excellent achievements through the years. I was leaving behind a close-knit organization composed of men and women who were as teary-eyed as I was, days before I departed. I felt as if I stood close to God when I was near them.

I was leaving with a heavy heart not just because of them, but because of the large accountability I now shared with my wife. I felt shame and remorse for the hurt we had inflicted on innocent people. What was especially pulling me down was the question of how we were going to repair the material destruction wrought by such misdeed. How shall we address the pain suffered by persons whose trust we violated?

Am I justified to say that the melon-sized faith we had in the power of God revealed to us three months ago, unceremoniously shrunk into mustard seed-size in the middle of this storm? In Luke 17:6, Jesus said, *"If you have faith as small as a mustard seed, you can say to this mulberry tree, 'Be uprooted and planted in the sea', and it will obey you."* Our faith in Him, regardless of how small it is, empowers us to even move mountains? I waived my chances of winning in the lottery since then.

God will provide.

RIDING THE STORM

My transfer to Negros Occidental, based in Bacolod City, took place in the summer of 1992. It encompassed a wider territory that offered a new set of challenges for me and my new team. I faced the new chapter in my professional life with readiness and enthusiasm. I felt blessed for my natural love for work. But, the dark monster of the past kept tagging at my side and gnawed at my being like an ugly rat. Its unrelenting attacks threatened to diminish the luster of the present and bring unimaginable destruction to my family's future.

I know where my strength lies. I can stretch my patience and remain calm up to an extreme point during critical times. I am slow to anger. I can stand solid even as I suffer in silence in the face of an emotional turbulence. I can tell you now with confidence: *the ultimate test on one man's character will always center on the strongest area of his personality*. Finally then, that man will be measured on the basis of how he responds to the test. I was tested on how long I would be able to stretch my patience and maintain the positive side of my character in that desperate hour. I was being measured to determine if I could fully ride out the storm like a sturdy tree, or snap like a dry twig under the rain. *Will the ugly rat be able to score a major point?*

Within one year in my new assignment, I earned a promotion. Barely 6 months into that promotion, my Division Head, Mr. Robert Cortez, told me about yet another promotion in rank he was granting me. With much appreciation and respect for him, I asked Mr. Cortez to please hold my promotion in abeyance as I felt it was too much of a blessing for me to be promoted by him twice within a year! I pledged I would continue to do my best to keep his trust in me alive, until I felt I was prepared to have *that* promotion again. Mr. Cortez was generous enough to understand and he followed my wish. Well, as it happened, despite all the hard work and dedication I showed for my job,

I never again earned any kind of promotion until I retired from service 9 years later. Lesson learned: Don't turn your back when opportunity comes knocking at your door because, as they say, lightning strikes only once! *God bless Mr. Cortez and his loved ones.*

I was leading a productive professional life, but vestiges of the past refused to leave me. The Bacolod City Sherriff had now assumed the task of running after my wife to collect. I had to overcome the diminishing effects on my sensibilities as I haggled with the City Sherriff for more time. My desperation pushed me to spend hard-earned money to send my wife off to Hongkong for overseas employment, but she was back in two weeks after her visa expired. Early in my adult life, I resolved never to get involved in a mess and avoid problems with the law. Now, here I was deeply entangled with men of the law. Irony of ironies. *Where do I go from here?*

The Lender in Roxas City was desperate to collect the balance of P230,000 to clean off the account. I was at my wit's end thinking about what to do next. All our 5 children were in high school and college. My monthly salary could give us the fund only for our daily sustenance. What we urgently needed right then was an extra source where we could tap P230,000 cash to end the ordeal.

The answer came in a dream.

I had a strange kind of dream that came at 4 in the morning. This is usually the time when my sleep is at its deepest and my dreams are at their clearest. In my dream, I was looking down at Nena Ong who was looking up at me as if she was trying to say something I could not figure out. It was different from my other dreams that do not leave an indelible imprint in my mind. It seemed so real, almost like a portrait left frozen inside my head totally devoid of words, but which contained a message I yet could not understand.

It didn't take long for me to learn the real message of that dream. At about 6, or barely 2 hours after having that dream, our telephone rang. I picked it up and heard the voice of Nena Ong at the opposite end! As I go back to that early-morning call, I can clearly remember what Nena Ong said to me, who used to call me by my nickname.

> "Land (me), Tim (the Lender) told me yesterday she is including you in her charges against Ikit (my wife) as an accessory to the crime. That is not fair because I know you are innocent. So, I was thinking about you early this morning (the precise moment when I had the dream) out of pity. I have talked with Toto (her husband, Vicente, Jr.) just now. We agreed to pay the outstanding balance of Mariquit's account of P230,000 as soon as the bank opens today. You don't have to worry anymore. You can pay us back the amount anytime you will have the funds to pay for it in the future."

If you were in my place, how would you have reacted? How would you present yourself before your life-saver who was far out of physical touch? Maybe, just as I did. With mixed feelings of surprise, disbelief and humility that came deep from within my soul and my heart, I simply said *"Nens, thank you very much!"* I broke down. I could hardly control myself and I wept. Tears kept welling down in silence even while I was under the bathroom shower and getting ready for work. I told my wife about what had just happened. I left home for work that morning with my wife still wide-eyed and smiling. She resolved not to do what she had done ever again.

Almost instantly, the heavy weight I'd been carrying around for several months was lifted off my chest. I pay tribute to the person who came in to pull me up when the whole world seemed to crumble in front of me. Nena Ong had been used for the *second time* by God to be the living instrument in bringing the sun back into my life. The *first time* was during my daughter's miraculous healing. True friends are indeed like diamonds. Precious and rare.

It was the 17th century physicist, Sir Isaac Newton, who said, *"If I have seen a little farther, it is by standing on the shoulders of giants."* I couldn't have overcome the steepest obstacles that blocked my path without the help of a **giant**. Today, I continue to march in cadence with the man who prayed: *"Lord, help me to become a friend who doesn't run when my friends are in need. Give me the courage to stand by them, the wisdom to know what to say, and the ability to serve them."* Lord, help me to become like Nena and Toto Ong. Amen.

True to her word, Nena paid off the balance of my wife's outstanding liability on the day and at the hour she gave me her word it would be done. I was finally free of the restraining shackles of our past and I praised God for this continuing string of miracles taking place in my life. Midnight had passed. The sunrise had signaled a new beginning! Bit by bit I managed to extract small amounts from my bonuses and basic income and pay back Nena the amount she generously lent us at the moment of the greatest need. Not even a cent was charged by them as interest. I can claim without doubt that I had the good fortune to come into close contact with a living saint in my life during my brief sojourn on this earth.

The days had brightened up once again. My wife and I led normal lives of career couples. All our 5 children were in school. One day, I had another dream happening at 4 am. It left me puzzled about its meaning again. In my dream, I was beholding a living **Pillar of Water** planted in the ocean, with its top end reaching the sky. It was "alive" because the massive foot of that watery column was gurgling and bubbling. The vertical body of the pillar was pulsating with its watery veins as it stood firm, impaling the sky. After gathering the details of that vision, I woke up with a start and wondered.

I took the element of water to mean life at its best, as I positively pointed to the *Water of Life* as my reference. Soon I had the chance to talk to Nena Ong over the telephone and ask her about her opinion. She called back the following day to share with me the idea she got from her discussion with her eldest son, Dandi, about the dream. As interpreted by them, my dream pointed to the coming days of more challenges and *sacrifices* yet in store for me! I expressed my protest, but took note of the message again carefully. After all the trials and agony we went through, did I not deserve a real good break from God that time around? Who would be proven right? Unfortunately I was proven *wrong* as events unfolded. My next venue for scourging was my own workplace.

THE WATER TEST

The nature of my job brought with it a high level of stress. There was a big challenge in my mandate to develop an effective manpower line-up with cutting-edge ability to sell an intangible product in the marketplace: *life insurance*. We attained growth marks annually, but we consistently failed to realize the high production goals assigned to my District and our West Visayas Region. Our Senior Personnel conceived of a way to enable the company to look good in figures, but promised to diminish its attribute of self-respect simply because it was not openly authorized by the top management in the first place. In our region, it was dubbed *Operation Lambat*. Other regions came up with their own tag names.

The dynamics of *Operation Lambat* sounded as gross as frying the company in its own fat. Our unit managers, and any licensed agent they recommend, would be granted cash advances that would be used to pay for the insurance premiums of new insurance policies they must purchase for their family members. Liquidation of these cash advances shall be made by retaining the incomes of the agents from their future sales. Immediate result would be increased productivity for everyone, with not a drop of honest sweat having been invested by anybody in such an effort. The company will then be exposed to a great degree of risk from uncollected advances granted to its agency force.

Posthaste, I called for a meeting with my field managers and solicited feedback from them. It was their consensus that *Operation Lambat* is a low-blow strategy to improve performance, a debasing tactic that will work against the morale of real performers. I agreed with them, and we decided not to implement *Operation Lambat* in our District. My immediate superiors were frustrated by our action, and I became one guy eased out of the team. I have been branded and treated like a black sheep from that moment onward.

Our District's performance suffered in comparison with that of the other Districts that went full-swing with *Operation Lambat*. Eventually, having been forced to save face, we gave in to the pressure and went with the throng on a limited volume during the closing weeks of the operation. I earned the reputation of being a bad team-player among my superiors and my peers on account of that incident.

The lid on *Operation Lambat* blew open when my District was scheduled for a routine internal audit, and the record of unjustified massive cash withdrawals by our sales force was discovered. I was made to explain. So, I did. Exposure of the operation into the open was blamed by my detractors on me. They wrongly accused me of being the one responsible for asking our company auditor to do an audit of our District for my supposed ill motive of exposing *Operation Lambat*! Lies and deception truly exist in both low and high places where men are so obsessed with worldly concerns. I'd been marked ripe for slaughter anytime they pleased. "*God, save me!*" I cried.

Every one of us, middle managers, who were tainted with *Operation Lambat* were meted with a few days' suspension without pay. Surprisingly, two of those who were within my circle earned their promotion.

I was called back with an assignment to Iloilo City in the early summer of 1996. I was now under my new bosses whose iron-fisted style of management did not fit well with the marketing norm. The mark of *Operation Lambat* was emblazoned flat on their foreheads.

MY EXILE

Recently I came across a Biblical verse that fit perfectly into Nena & Dandi Ong's interpretation of the **Pillar of Water** that appeared in my dream. I quote Isaiah 43:1-2, "*Do not fear for I have called you by name. You are mine! When you pass through the waters, I will be with you. When you pass through the rivers, they will not drown you. When you walk through the fire, it will not destroy you. The flame will not burn you.*"

The Biblical footnote explains that "*pass through the waters*" means difficult problems, while "*walk through the fire*" refers to life's fiery trials. I went through all this, including wading "*through the rivers*" whose meaning may well encompass the various degrees of trials and misery one man can go through, still to emerge whole in one piece only by the grace of God.

I considered my assignment in Iloilo City to be a happy occasion. I looked forward to working closely again with people I've known for quite a long time in my familiar terrain. However, I had barely warmed my seat when I was given the order to report to Surigao City, starting in January 1997. The only question I managed to ask my Division Head then was,

"Where is that place?" Surigao City turned out to be a rugged, small-sized city used as reference point for incoming typhoons by weather forecasters.

When the news broke out, my immediate reaction was to raise the white flag and leave my job. On second thought I pondered over that idea: *Where will I go? My three children are still in school. And if I go, I shall be missing the opportunity to redeem myself before the presence of my detractors while they sit comfortably in their high positions, amply rewarded and virtually untouched?* I made my decision to hold the fort and face the dragons. I did not realize then, that my superiors purposely assigned me to Surigao City so that I might be prompted to resign from my job in no time at all!

With me not even lifting a finger at all for my cause, the whole West Visayas Region went up in arms on my behalf. Letters of appeal for my retention were sent to the President, individually and in groups per District Office (Iloilo, Bacolod, Roxas), including those of employees. But they were all summarily ignored. Those letters to the President were later delivered to me by the Office of the President instead, in a bunch, for my safe-keeping. I still have them in an album for posterity. Even our President believed the version my superiors gave him that it was through my own instigation that the whole Region came up with those letters of appeal to support me. What chances did I have for redemption? Did I deserve crucifixion in the name of team-play?

Christmas 1996 was the blackest Christmas we experienced as a family. It will remain forever seared in my memory as such. Surigao City, despite its rugged beauty and promise of adventure, delivered the stark message of moral breakdown within our organization and corporate insensitivity meted out to me. Even while in the middle of a crowd, I felt so alone. God stood as my companion even into the lowest pit of my desperation. I faltered, but I refused to fall.

A very good friend from Surigao City, Clem Sykimte, was surprised to see me there. He asked me the question, "Why are you here? Don't you know that Surigao City is known to be the graveyard of **Insular Life**?" I replied, "Clem, please help me make Surigao City become the place of my **resurrection**." And he did, together with new-found friends we trained and developed to lead productive lives in Surigao City!

Simultaneous with my transfer to Surigao City, the single person who was mainly responsible for my woes, was also transferred to Davao City, a major regional center in our corporate map. It was surely a gesture of promotion for his "job well done".

I stayed for a total of 1 year and 7 months in Surigao City. I used to kid my wife by telling her that I'd be away from home most of the time as I trained her how to live the life of a widow. There were many weekends when I would feel homesick and heart-broken as I had nothing else to do. I would merely stay in my room and shed tears of my loneliness before God. An outsider during his first visit to Surigao City described the place early in 1997 as "the place where God shouted, but nobody listened:" *Lord, what am I doing here? I feel so wasted and abused. But, I came here with a mission. I have to pay for the price of fairness and truth. I must go on.*

I felt the surge of spirituality embrace me as I began going out with my group to church, regardless of sect, on weekends. I learned how to sing and be touched by the songs of worship of our Protestant brothers and sisters. I went regularly to a Roman Catholic church in the city where I surrendered everything to God. I let go of all the pain, worry, resentment, anger and concern for my family. I brought them all before God as an offering. In their place, I opened my heart wide for my act of forgiveness to all those who did me harm.

I would commune with God in this manner as I wept in silence: *"Lord, thank you for the blessings you've showered on us. Allow me to open up my heart to You. I do this without reservation, as I forgive all those who have hurt me and my family. From deep inside my heart, I forgive all of them. May You bless them as You continue to bless me and make us all become better persons."* I'd then proceed to mention the names of those persons who did me wrong, and open-heartedly forgave them – *every single one of them.*

Years ago, I relied on hard work alone to make things happen. This time around, I gloried in our achievement of having moved mountains through *faith* (in God and in ourselves), fortified with hard work. I began operations in Surigao City in January 1997 with only 5 licensed underwriters, and ended the year with 18. We increased our productivity rate by a formidable 307% over that of the previous year. We emerged to be the District that registered the highest growth rate for the year, nation-wide. My perception of the place changed dramatically: *Surigao City had become the place where a handful of people shouted, and God listened!*

In late 1997, during one of our quarterly meetings of Managers held in Cagayan de Oro City, the regional seat for North Mindanao, our company President was present. The President asked me if I knew about the latest news on personnel movements. I was so out of touch of the current events that I went blank. I was then informed that the person who used to be my Regional Manager in Western Visayas was petitioned out of Davao City by our sales force there. So, he was this time called back to report to our Makati Head Office in a floating status. Before the appointed date of his recall came, however, he pulled a fast one by resigning from service in a huff. He then joined the ranks of our industry competitor. He transferred employment from one insurance company to another within a few years, before he had a stroke in his early 40's. Our Division Head, who supported him, was somehow encouraged to leave the service after a while, for reasons quite unknown to me up to this day. *God bless them and their loved ones.*

Our higher management could now have understood clearly who had been on the side of truth ever since. By the middle of 1998, I was called upon to handle the new position of Regional Administrative Manager in San Fernando, Pampanga. It was a job not related to marketing anymore; hence, it would come with a reduced amount of stress. But, the assignment would still place me far away from my family. So, I refused the offer, which I regretted so much a few years later. Had I accepted that offer, I could have stayed longer with the company and completed my tour of duty after having been posted to all three national regions of Luzon, Visayas and Mindanao.

I was then elevated to the position of Regional Head of North Mindanao based in Cagayan de Oro City. My other highly-ranked superiors who were part of the team that engineered my momentary downfall must have felt bitter while licking their wounds after losing their war. Yet, even until the time I left the service 3 years later, no one came forward to offer their apologies. I prayed and worked for my salvation and vindication. Through God's grace and my faithfulness, I emerged badly scarred but victorious in the end. *The source of my strength is God.*

Undoubtedly, Surigao City has become my place of resurrection and the unlikely spot of my final vindication.

THISTLES BY THE WAYSIDE

From being a District Manager, I was granted the higher title of Regional Manager of North Mindanao, with Cagayan de Oro City as regional base in 1998. I still maintained the rank of Assistant Manager. This was the same rank I held since my posting in Bacolod City in 1992, until my optional retirement in 2001. The area entrusted to me was vast. The assignment gave me first-hand view of what Mindanao was during that period.

Mindanao was, and still is, truly a land of promise. Commerce and agriculture were flourishing. Fresh supply of fruits, vegetables and marine products was plentiful every day. The industrial sector was alive with activity spurred by whirring factories and manufacturing plants giving employment to local, as well as out-of-town residents. The fly in the ointment was, and still is, the recurring problem of insurgency.

One had to watch out for the deadly bombing forays of insurgents in unlikely places. The barge which I used to ride on during my trips from Iligan City to Ozamis City the previous week, would be the site of a bomb attack the following week that wrecked havoc on property and lives of innocent civilians. Buses would explode and leave some people dead or mangled. There was no guarantee of a safe passage when one went out on field visitations. The trip from Cagayan de Oro City to Surigao City, for instance, would take at least 6 hours one-way. The challenges were daunting. I was looking at the limitless potential in working hard with results, but I could feel that my time was running out. I am now slowly maturing at 48, going 49! I was romping on kilometers of high-risk real estate which some other people would have second thoughts of treading.

During one of my home visits to Iloilo City, my wife surprised me with her house renovation work she managed to undertake through her own initiative. It was an extension to the old house: a newly-tiled living room painted white with a hanging chandelier. It looked beautiful. Except that, firstly, we no longer owned the property after we sold it to my sister. Secondly, she had the renovation done wholly on borrowed money.

Thirdly, she had no funds to pay for it. Promptly, after a brief family conference, I decided to let go of our 3-year old car which I acquired through monthly salary deductions. It was a Toyota Corolla that barely reached 20,000 kilometers in mileage which I was forced to sell for P230,000. The fund was used to again totally pay off her account. It was a clean surgery. My emotional attachment to material possessions acquired through hard work no longer mattered. My three children who were still in college had to, henceforth, catch up with their daily school schedules through public transport. We all had to bite the bullet as we proceeded with our journey through life, rain or shine, straightaway and without hesitation. *The ugly rat remained scoreless!*

HOME AT LAST

My long trek home was about to end. After making an objective inventory of my current personal profile and firepower, I made a request to be finally assigned back to my home region in Western Visayas. The war was over, and the old soldier deserved to be sent back home.

I was then assigned as Regional Manager of West Visayas Region, based in Iloilo City, in the summer of 2000. Home at last! *Thank you, Sir, Mr. Ramon M. Cabrera!* I had left the place as a beaten soul 3 years before. Now, I had returned home a new man, with my full redemption in hand. *Lord, thank you ever so much!*

We were again looking up to a new sunrise, a new day for everyone. I was doing my work with my usual drive and enthusiasm. By December 2000, we were working on ending the year with a bang in our performance. I was going round the region – Roxas, Kalibo, Bacolod, Antique, Iloilo – like a man possessed. I simply ignored a bad case of coughing I was carrying around for a couple of weeks. I went to see a doctor who prescribed an anti-biotic drug that left me sleepless for a few nights, but didn't stop my coughing. I just kept on moving around while continuously awake for 24 hours straight.

One December dawn, I finally drifted off to forgetfulness while lying awake in bed the whole night, out of sheer exhaustion. I jerked awake at the sound of the church bell ringing for the *Aguinaldo Mass* as I felt a nasty kick inside my chest that left me gasping for breath. I panicked as I struggled to breathe in more air, but it was useless. I felt weak and I was breathing hard. Was I having a heart attack? Could this be the end?

If I finally leave my family for good, I'd be happy to see Shasha now pursuing a light career in sales, Bobok getting established in Antique, and only Junjun still in his final year in college. My wife shall be well taken care of by my package of beneficiary benefits from my employer. But at the moment, my wife and Shasha were rushing me on board the car to St. Paul's Hospital, with Junjun on the wheel. Lester was then secure in America, and Claudine settled in Roxas City with her own family.

After checking my vital signs, my physician declared: *No, it was not a heart attack, after all.* My lungs were very sick. I ignored them for so long. My heart was struggling so hard to maintain air pressure. I needed to start taking the correct medicines. My internal pipes were clogged. My whole body was crying for rest.

So, I stayed in the hospital for 3 days and caught up on rest and sleep. I was back at work after a couple of weeks, but I was not as good as the original anymore. I seemed to have lost my natural defenses against stress. My hands would start to turn cold without warning. Then, I developed anxiety attacks as the days wore on. I started to find it hard to regain my normal sleep pattern. That usually caused episodes of panic attacks. *The ugly rat was beginning to catch up on me?*

I felt claustrophobic – the fear of being confined in close and narrow spaces. I would now consciously close my eyes inside an airplane before take-off when the air-conditioning was controlled. I felt the urge of running out of my hotel room and be free outside to do I knew not what! Sometimes, even just a slight change in the barometer would trigger an attack. Something went wrong with how my neurons were behaving.

I went deeper into prayer when I was in the middle of the attacks. It worked! My focus would then be re-directed from the center of terror, to the calming embrace of prayer. *The Lord is my Shepherd. I shall fear no evil. I shall not want!* Then, I finally learned how to manage this disorder when I sought professional help from *Dr. Eufemio Sobrevega,* the husband of Dr. Epifania Sobrevega, now a successful *Neurosurgeon* at the Iloilo Doctors Hospital. He used to be Shasha's Neurologist in 1991. I consider myself totally recovered within two years (2000-2002) under his care. *Thank you, Doctor!*

What triggered my retirement from the corporate life? Junjun graduated as Computer Engineer at the University of San Agustin in April 2001. He was our youngest child we had to send to school. One of our main jobs as parents was somehow accomplished against all odds. Junjun was standing at the crossroads of his young life when we asked him what his plans were. He answered: *I wish to go to America and find my destiny there. But, I don't know my way around!*

It didn't take long for his mother and me to decide to retire from our jobs, and fly with him to New York City in June 2001. I was only 52, my wife was 51. We were in Houston, Texas, USA, as we watched on live TV the Twin Towers of the World Trade Center in New York being demolished by two commercial airplanes. September 11, 2001 saw the start of a new brand of terror that chilled the whole world.

When man feels hopeless, that's the time when he stops trying. We remained full of hope even after our retirement. I consider it a master stroke from God for us to have built a new house standing on a wider area than the one we lost. My retirement package took care of that. Our three children in America put up a common fund we used as down payment for a brand new car to replace the one we also lost. Shasha assumed the task of paying for the 4-year monthly installments (July 2007 to June 2011). Whatever material gains we had after we retired, I consider them to be gifts from God. *Thank you, Lord, for our loving children!*

I went through the highs and lows of human experience that delivered vital lessons in life. For every count of ignorance I lost, I found faith. The sunrises and sunsets we went through were but a series of survival tests we had to overcome for the enrichment of our character and the evolution of our spirit. One finally discovers he is just one link to the chain that gives continuity to life. As we stumble and fall during our walk, **Someone** comes along to raise us up and give us hope. Along the way, God's message is conveyed to us almost in an intimate whisper, telling us in loving confidence: *My child, my child, I Am with you always, even unto the end!*

So, how would one put an end to a story that has no end? I dare answer: *with a pause.* Someday, maybe a son, a daughter, a nephew or a niece, a grandchild, or even a friend shall find the passion to again pick up the thread and add further chapters to this story without an end.

Momentarily, I pause with the declaration: *everything happened as I have written.* Thanks be to God.

"The most beautiful people we have known are those who have known defeat, known suffering, known struggle, known loss, and have found their way out of the depths. These persons have an appreciation, a sensitivity and understanding of life that fills them with compassion, gentleness, and a deep loving concern. Beautiful people do not just happen."

-Elizabeth Kubler-Ross

In the middle of chaos during a *Magnitude 7* earthquake, a lady was observed to be standing unafraid in a street corner and looking skyward. No trace of fear or alarm showed in her face. Somebody called her up to take shelter in a nearby shade and asked, *"Are you not afraid of the earthquake?"*

She answered, *"No. I am just glad we have a God who is strong enough to shake the world like that!"*

Part 3

Glorifying the Mystery of God

Divinely inspired reflections and original poetry

Changing Of the Seasons

See the sparrows aim for the sky
Riding the wind no one knows why
Kissed by the summer's verdant view
To become next winter's sea of snow

- Rolando Y. Dy Buco

FIREFLIES ON THE MIND

*A*pril 30, 2008 breezed past without a trace. But, that date marked a milestone for the two of us, as my sweet bride and I notched another high point in our shared enterprise: Our 35th Wedding Anniversary!

The day was a dreary non-event. Not a candle was lighted. No *Red Ribbon* cake was sliced. Not even a stick of *watusi* bomb cracked. There lies, perhaps, the secret of why we've stayed long in the business: Our tendency to just take things in their stride. The day's significance earned casual notice through some strawberry-coated remarks, such as, *"Dear, 35 years na 'ta?"* Countered by, *"Daw kasan-o lang 'no?"* Then, back to the salt mines.

Our common enemy lurks ahead in ambush: Time.

⁂

I'M QUITE FOND of her, my wife, who's both my angel and my saint in the home front. I feel pampered. She does her chores all these years without complaints, as if she earned her degree from a University: Major in Culinary Arts, Lavation, and Floral Gardening with honors! My *Angel Kusinera* and my *Saint Labandera.* Need I ask for more?

Her talents are varied and latent. She retains part of her naiveté which I found endearing right from the start. It's because of her brittle vulnerability that she remains to be my life's supreme challenge as we move past our prime.

⁂

EVERY MORNING I make it my practice to murmur words of thanks to God for everything granted to us for 17 years now (1991-2008). I was transformed into becoming a *new* man. The

42 years prior to that period (1949-1991), I stood like an arrogant fool before the eyes of God.

I'm so blessed by God in my ordinary life and I realize it more only now. I'm blessed by God with a wife who isn't perfect. She's a woman of beauty in my eyes, in her high elements in many places, while not as wise in others.

I also refuse to hate myself every time I'm confronted with my own failures and mistakes. We all experience some glitches along the way because perfection isn't the quality labeled in the package we were tucked inside with when we arrived, unless, of course, one chooses to come with batteries and fully computerized?

❧

WE'RE so blessed by God with 5 children who possess intriguing personality types. This made me realize there's no way to stem the ebb and flow of life, even if at 29 I had already been vasectomized. Five colorful kids walking through the avenue of life in search of their own Edens, turning our world vibrant and bright. Plus, a bonus of nine healthy and sweet-smelling grandchildren to date!

As Wakit (my wife's nickname) counts 59 in 2009 and as I, Bando (my nickname), turn 60, we welcome the new wrinkles on our foreheads and our increasing crown of grey. We don't hold an exclusive franchise to the element of time as years advance, but the matter about age is only in the mind. Notwithstanding the onslaught of rising cholesterols and recurring muscle pains in our varied anatomical regions, the mind may yet transcend known physical limits and transport us to newer heights.

We can still break into giggles and unsuppressed laughter as we recall funny times past, and make happier moments last.

Thank you, our children, for keeping us company in our walk. This enterprise remains strong as it was built to last and to stand fast for life.

1986. (l-r) Rolando Jr., Roland Lester, Credence, Mommy (Wakit), Daddy (Bando), Melody & Claudine Marie.

CHRISTMAS TOGETHER

The thought sank in like a slithering earthworm
During the usual walk one cold December morn
Off the beaten way down San Gregorio home
Of young dreams made and memories born.

Christmas old was excitement laden
Christmas now doesn't come the same
We yearn to see the memorable sparkles
In the eyes of our children blending, as they were
Focused on tinsel gifts soon ripped and torn.

We dream of Christmases past and tender years then
When Claudine as a tot, stood over her brood
        like a clucking hen would
Little Lester with wrinkled nose so cute, now ready to emote
Bright Melody bubbled with delight
        while learning how to walk
Lola's kid, Bobok, wailed for hours
        in search of his "Thermos", and
Cuddly Junjun cool in a corner
        armed with charm, soulful and dolorous.

By His Touch

Christmas of youth meant mangled Yuletide carols
Games and heaps of plastic toys gay wrappers shorn
Mommy would set the mood for the evening
As she maintained order in her kitchen domain
Soon, holiday food will make the table groan
As little tummies are filled for the coming pandemonium.

The Nativity was re-enacted amid giggles and sneers
Lines spoken in mechanical fashion,
     heavy with wide-eyed anticipation
"Let the games begin!" Daddy hollered
Off they went on a Treasure Hunt roam
Nanay Meling crawled, Mommy Inday swooned.

Christmas today may look and sound the same
Except for the children's faces now duly transformed
People rushing through the bargain avenues, croak and moan
Where to buy? What to wrap? What to cook? When to stop?
Boundless joy and endless thrills, the mood is merry and festive
The spirit of love alive to last 'til the next season.

Wakit is now 55, and Bando 56
Things change as they can't be the same again
Life swings us up, bangs us down in roller-coaster ride fashion
That leaves one feeling ill after a spin, well again, then ill again
Morning aerobics made Bando realize that at his age now
If God really wanted him to touch his toes as he bends
HE would have put them up on his knees then!
Notwithstanding the subtraction, we insist without question
We are truly blessed by Him
We thank the Lord for the shower of blessings that came
After tests and trials of nightmares made

Into sweet-tasting dreams re-formed.

The far-reaching embrace of Christmas now comes
From once smelly and funny kids whose acts of love convey
The message: we are remembered across miles of void
From a nearby corner, to half-a-globe away
Oh yes, making the old guys merry,
    as they both feel oh, so teary!
Allow the magic, fun, warmth and the love
    of old Christmases reign:
A BLESSED CHRISTMAS TO YOU ALL,
DEAR CHILDREN, PRAY LET OUR LOVE REMAIN!

My Life in Two Acts

ACT 1

Christmas 2009 comes as another time for reflection. I am on the 6th decade of my life, with Wakit huffing hot behind my neck and counting 59.

At 60, my world has turned upside down. As a kid then, I enjoyed half-rate rides on buses, jeeps, ferris wheels and even when paying entrance into cinemas with *Nay Meling* to watch her favorite *Tagalog* movie showing downtown. Today, I take pleasure in flashing off my senior citizen card on fast-food and grocery counters, or a Japanese all-you-can-eat restaurant and be extended with a 20% discount on gross charges. Amazingly now, my smart-looking 8-year old grandson is being charged a full-rate on everything, including entering cinemas to watch his cartoons yak or Michael Jackson roll!

Hurray for the simple joys of ageing! Accursed is he who is confronted with the mounting travails of youth!

Thank you, Lord, for the gift of our children who make us feel blessed for the value of life lived yesterday – today and tomorrow. Without them, where could we be? Have we ever done anything so outstandingly pleasing before the eyes of God to deserve this?

The answers may yet be forthcoming as one recalls a line from the movie, "Sound Of Music" that said, *"Somewhere in my youth or childhood, I could have done something good!"* Today, I assume the role of the nanny-heroine named Maria (Julie Andrews), who simply couldn't stop wondering what on earth had she done to deserve the favorable twist happening in her life. Life's mystery amazes me without end.

Proverbs 20:7 states: *"The righteous man walks in his integrity, his children are blessed after him."* Does this provide part of the answer to the question?

ACT 2

The first-half of my life was replete with high-value pursuits devoted to family-building. The kids were growing up fast. Their diverse needs must be addressed with urgency: physical, emotional, intellectual, spiritual.

The spiritual aspect, by impulse, came in last. Not by design, even as I encountered in one of my book readings in school, Karl Marx, who said something like man has to satisfy his physical needs first before he can attend to things spiritual in nature. Did he nail it right?

Hebrews 11:6. *"Without faith it is impossible to please Him, for he who comes to God must believe that He is, and that He is a rewarder of those who diligently seek Him."*

It was much later when I realized deep within me that I was longing for God. My feeling of emptiness heightened as I began asking myself questions about my real purpose of existence here on earth. I'm surely not the first, nor the last person who was, or will be confronted by earth-centered conundrums such as this one. So, how did I come across the answer?

In the Holy Bible, we read about Jesus saying, *"Knock and you shall be opened, ask and you shall be given, seek and you shall find."* Only searchers become finders. If you don't seek, then you shall not find. But, don't expect to find the answer to your questions sleekly bound in logic. Don't even put too much weight on human intelligence as we know it to be.

Wisdom comes along at a time when you least expect it. It is delivered to you in God's own time and not by your own measure. My life's experiences made me realize that God grants divine revelation not only among His saints, but even among the doubters in our midst. Jesus allowed His wound to be touched first and only by a doubting Thomas, remember?

So, we are blessed by God to be revived by His healing touch. Fifteen years ago, I dreamed of a living pillar of water that rose up to the sky. It warned me of impending trials and agony yet to come along my way. I experienced the restorative power of compassion expressed by a friend who pulled me up from a dark hole, hopeless and beaten. I went through repeated small deaths, but I regained life each time.

Today, I experience joy and serenity as I look up to my children who went through with us in our passage full of life's unscheduled stops and turns. They are our children who brim with youthful energy, hope and vision just as we were, my wife and I, during the best and the worst of times. I, therefore, proclaim this second-half of my life replete with visions of triumph, victory and stripes earned from our major battles won.

Thank you, oh Lord, for this gift of LIFE!

WHAT THE FUTURE HOLDS

Just a month ago, on December 8th, 2010, I was working on the finishing pages of my manuscript when the phone rang. Shasha herself was on the phone from her home in California, USA. She sounded calm and at peace with herself, but sad.

The feeling was familiar. It was as if I was drawn back into the vortex of strange events taking place 19 years ago, in November 1991. It was as if I was pushed once again into the center of a new playing field and made to play defense in a game whose rules I know nothing about.

She was telling me over the phone that she had just been diagnosed with breast cancer. Our world was badly shaken up again by the news. She was only 34. *Why cancer? Why now?*

I could feel nothing but shock while thinking about how a fulfilling young life may be cruelly altered by the presence of a treacherous intruder as cancer. What immediately crossed my mind was an old quote saying, *"Stay close to your friends, but closer to your enemies."* The best way to overcome the enemy is to know him up close.

In a couple of weeks after that call, I had more grasp about the "enemy" as I read through two books lent to me by a good friend, Mr. Ramon Patrick "Bong" Mabilog, whose wife succumbed to Stage 4 Breast Cancer three years before. The books were: *Journeys with the Cancer Conqueror* and *The Complete Cancer Cleanse*. They introduced ideas on how best to approach the disease on its own terms through identified physical, emotional and spiritual channels of healing: Body, Mind, Spirit.

What am I looking at in the future?

Shasha certainly held the edge. She remained firm in her strong faith in God Who heals. She instantly embarked on a new diet program focused on food choices best for her. She had resolved to get rid of emotional toxins that have profound effects on her health. In brief, she was learning how to enjoy life fully and opened herself up to the soul-cleansing principles of unconditional love. Will she be able to regain her good health? I am positive!

As she picks up new knowledge about life, I am motivated by love to learn much from her. James 5:16 says, *"Pray for one another, that you may be healed."* We are praying without ceasing. After all, it's only God Who has the power to turn a mess into a message!

I may be justified in my belief that the next testimony we will read about God's wonderful gifts will come from no other person than Shasha herself. God's rich and endless treasures are waiting to be discovered.

Together we search.

June 2011. Shasha at 20 yrs & 7 months after her healing, flanked by Dad and Mom, in her home in Concord, CA (USA).

SELECTED HEALING VERSES FROM THE BIBLE

John 10:10. "*The thief does not come except to steal, and to kill, and to destroy. I have come that (you) may have life, and that (you) may have it more abundantly.*" (The devil wants to kill you; God wants to heal.)

Matthew 8:2, 3. "*Lord, if You are willing, You can make me clean. And Jesus said these simple words, I am willing: be cleansed.*" (It is God's will for you to be healed.)

Exodus 23:5. "*So you shall serve the Lord your God, and He will bless your bread and your water. And I will take sickness away from the midst of you.*" (Serve the Lord and healing will be yours.)

Deuteronomy 7:15. "*And the Lord will take away from you all sickness, and will afflict you with none of the terrible diseases of Egypt which you have known, but will lay them on all those who hate you.*" (God takes ALL sickness away from you.)

Psalm 107:20. *"He sent His Word and healed them, and delivered them from their destructions."* (God's Word is healing.)

Psalm 118:17. *"I shall not die, but live, and declare the works of the Lord."* (God wants you to live with a purpose.)

Jeremiah 30:17. *"For I will restore health to you and heal you of your wounds."* (God will restore your health.)

Matthew 18:19. *"Again I say to you that if two of you agree on earth concerning anything that they ask, it will be done for them by My Father in heaven."* (Agree with someone, your wife or husband, for your healing. Don't allow negative thoughts to come between you.)

Mark 11:24. *"Therefore I say to you, whatever things you ask when you pray, believe that you receive them, and you will have them."* (Believe, and you will receive.)

Mark 16: 17, 18. *"And these signs shall follow those who believe… they will lay hands on the sick, and they will recover."* (Have someone lay hands on you for healing.)

John 9:31. *"If anyone is a worshipper of God and does His will, He hears him.* (Worship God. Say, "Jesus I love You and I worship You. I come before You today, thanking You that your word hasn't changed.")

Joel 3:10. *"Let the weak say, 'I am strong'."* (Find strength in God and His Word. When you feel weak, repeat this verse and it will strengthen you.)

James 5:14, 15. *"Is anyone among you sick? Let him call for the elders of the church, and let them pray over him, anointing them with oil in the name of the Lord. And the prayer of faith will save the sick, and the Lord will raise him up."* (Be anointed with oil, or holy water, by a Christian who believes in healing.)

2 Timothy 1:7. *"For God has not given us a spirit of fear but of power and of love and of a sound mind."* (Fear is not of God. Rebuke it!)

Revelation 12:11. *"And they overcame him by the blood of the Lamb and by the word of their testimony."* (Give testimony of your healing.)

Nahum 1:9. *"Affliction will not rise up a second time."* (Your sickness will leave and not come back again.)

ACKNOWLEDGEMENTS

I join with my wife, Mariquit, in expressing my gratitude for the assistance I received from a few people during the course of writing this little book.

THANK YOU!

My loving son, Roland Lester B. Dy Buco and his beautiful wife, Christina, for the wonderful gift of a Sony VAIO laptop during my one-month stay with them in Torrance, California, USA, in February 2010. That planted the seed of an idea that slowly blossomed into becoming this book you are now holding in your hands;

My doting grandson, Antonio D. Chu, IV, for providing me with the technical support in mastering my laptop as I ran through this project, from beginning to end (Philippines);

My highly supportive son-in-law, Engr. Moises S. Malong, III, for being generous with his time he shared with me in the preparation of the final draft of the manuscript (Concord, California, USA);

My multi-talented nephew, Atty. Edward James A. Dy Buco, for standing as my legal adviser and for shedding a few tears with his dearest wife, Engr. Ianne C. Dy Buco, while reading through my manuscript;

My classmate, Rhoda Galindo Gutierrez of Sunnyvale, California, USA. She is the lamb who feeds contentedly on the green pastures of the Lord. Events conspired for her to get hold of a copy of the manuscript. Providentially, she held the mystical key that opened the way for this book to see print here. She doesn't believe in accidents.

My **Creator**, my **Source** of life. **He** allowed us time and space to go through the amazing process of having experienced **Perfect Love** during our brief sojourn on planet Earth. All the glory goes back to **Him**.

To everyone else, I give you all my eternal gratitude.

ABOUT THE AUTHOR

Rolando Yap Dy Buco was born in 1949 in Culasi, Antique in the central region of the Philippines. He obtained his Bachelor of Arts in Political Science at the University of San Agustin, Iloilo City in 1972, where he served as editor of the campus paper for 2 years. His 31-year career in the life insurance industry brought him close into understanding the innate human desire for the intangibles. His unplanned early retirement provided him with time enough to reflect and write down long-nurtured thoughts about his own reasons for life. *By His Touch* is his first vehicle that invites the reader to join him to stand witness to his remarkable journey of faith.

In Memoriam

HILDA VERONICA *(Nena)* **DIOSO ONG**
9 July 1942 – 18 December 2005
A faithful child of God, devoted wife and mother,
a loving friend, mentor and confidant

&

VICENTE *(Toto)* **UY KIMPANG ONG, JR.**
21 March 1938 – 23 August 2006
A true friend and brother we treasure so much